Customs Around the World

GAMES
Around the World

by Lindsay Shaffer

Raintree is an imprint of Capstone Global Library Limited, a company incorporated in England and Wales having its registered office at 264 Banbury Road, Oxford, OX2 7DY – Registered company number: 6695582

www.raintree.co.uk
myorders@raintree.co.uk

Text © Capstone Global Library Limited 2021
The moral rights of the proprietor have been asserted.

All rights reserved. No part of this publication may be reproduced in any form or by any means (including photocopying or storing it in any medium by electronic means and whether or not transiently or incidentally to some other use of this publication) without the written permission of the copyright owner, except in accordance with the provisions of the Copyright, Designs and Patents Act 1988 or under the terms of a licence issued by the Copyright Licensing Agency, Barnard's Inn, 86 Fetter Lane, London, EC4A 1EN (www.cla.co.uk). Applications for the copyright owner's written permission should be addressed to the publisher.

Edited by Gena Chester
Designed by Julie Peters
Original illustrations © Capstone Global Library Limited 2021
Picture research by Jo Miller
Production by Spencer Rosio
Originated by Capstone Global Library Ltd
Printed and bound in India

978 1 3982 0260 3 (hardback)
978 1 3982 0259 7 (paperback)

British Library Cataloguing in Publication Data
A full catalogue record for this book is available from the British Library.

Acknowledgements
We would like to thank the following for permission to reproduce photographs: Capstone Studio: Karon Dubke, 9; Getty Images: ViewStock, 7; Newscom:, Harry M. Walker, 23; Shutterstock: Africa Studio, Cover, Ami Parikh, 12–13, dani shlom, 28, GMMaria, 11, i_am_zews, 25, Monkey Business Images, 1, Natalya Erofeeva, 27, NIKS ADS, 5, Peruphotart, 15, Sergey Novikov, 21, XiXinXing, 17; Wikimedia: Benebiankie, 19. Design elements: Capstone; Shutterstock: Stawek (map), VLADGRIN

Every effort has been made to contact copyright holders of material reproduced in this book. Any omissions will be rectified in subsequent printings if notice is given to the publisher.

All the internet addresses (URLs) given in this book were valid at the time of going to press. However, due to the dynamic nature of the internet, some addresses may have changed, or sites may have changed or ceased to exist since publication. While the author and publisher regret any inconvenience this may cause readers, no responsibility for any such changes can be accepted by either the author or the publisher.

CONTENTS

Games around the world 4
Chasing games 6
Throwing games 10
Hide and seek games 16
Sports 20
Board games 24

Map 29
Glossary 30
Find out more 31
Index 32

Words in **bold** are in the glossary.

GAMES AROUND THE WORLD

People around the world love playing games. What sort of games do you like to play?

Games bring people together. They help us connect with our friends and family. They also help us make new friends.

Some games make us laugh. Other games **challenge** us. They teach us new skills. They give us a fun way to **practise** skills too!

Children in India playing cricket

CHASING GAMES

Have you ever run after a friend in a game of tag? Chasing games are played in many places. In China, children play catch the dragon's tail. A group of children stand in a line. They place their hands on the child in front of them.

The child in front runs to tag the child at the back. The others hold on tight! They laugh and shout. The line twists and turns. Will the dragon catch its tail?

Children in Greece play another type of tag. They call the game *agalmata*. This means "statue" in Greek.

One player is chosen to be it. He covers his eyes and counts to 10 or higher. The other players spread out. He shouts, "Agalmata!" The other players freeze. They try to look like statues. They must be careful not to move. If they do, the boy who is it can tag them!

THROWING GAMES

Some children play catch with a ball. Others throw fruit! In Israel, children throw apricot **stones**. During a game, a stone sails through the air. It drops through a small hole in the top of a shoebox. "Ten points!" cries the girl who threw it. Her brother hands her ten stones, or go-gos.

apricot stone

Next, he throws a go-go towards another shoebox. It lands in a larger hole. "Five points!" he shouts. His sister gives him five go-gos. Whoever earns the most go-gos wins the game of go-go-im!

In Australia, children play a game called down down down. Two players stand a few metres apart. They throw a ball back and forth. They try hard not to drop it. A player who drops the ball must drop down. After one drop, the player rests on one knee.

Each drop brings the player closer to the ground. Players may end up on both knees. They may even lie on their chins! The most upright player wins the game.

In Peru, people play *sapo*. This means "toad" in Spanish. First, they set up a large box. The top of the box is covered in holes. A metal toad sits in the middle. The toad's mouth is open.

Players take turns throwing coins towards the box. They get points when a coin lands in a hole. The player who throws a coin into the toad's mouth wins the game. Which throwing game do you want to play?

HIDE AND SEEK GAMES

Children play searching games all around the world. In the United States, children play hide-and-seek. To play, a child closes his eyes. He counts to 20. Other players run away while he is counting. They hide.

"Ready or not, here I come!" shouts the counter. Now, he must find his friends. The last child found wins the game!

Children in Ghana play pilolo. The word *pilolo* means "time to search for". Children form a group. One child is the leader. Leaders hide small objects. Another child keeps the time. Timekeepers stand by a finish line and decide who wins.

To start, the leader shouts, "*Pilolo!*" The others search for the objects. They race to find the objects first. Once a child finds one, she runs it past the finish line. The first child to cross wins the game. Would you want to be a timekeeper, leader or racer?

SPORTS

What sports are played around the world? In Sweden, children play table tennis. Have you ever played?

Two people stand at the ends of a large table. Each player holds a wooden paddle. A short net sits across the middle of the table. It **divides** the table into two sides.

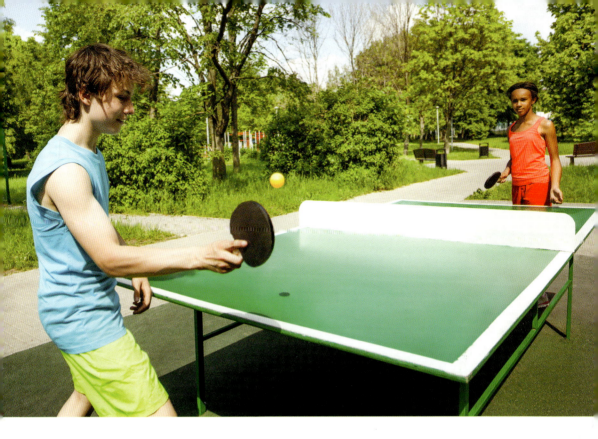

One player tosses a small white ball into the air. Then, she hits the ball with her paddle. The ball bounces over the net. It must land on the other side. The other player swings his paddle. He aims for the ball. He misses! The first player scores. The player who scores 11 points first wins.

Inuit tribes in Alaska and Canada play stick pull. There are also stick-pull **competitions**. The sport needs two people. They sit on the floor facing each other. The bottoms of their feet must touch. All hands must be on the stick. And then they pull.

Players can win in two ways. They pull the stick so hard the other player comes up off the floor. Or they pull so hard the other player falls over.

A stick pull competition in Anchorage, Alaska

BOARD GAMES

You need **strategy** to win most board games. People in Egypt use it when they play mancala. The board is lined with twelve small pockets. Four stones rest in each pocket. Two larger, empty pockets are at each end. These are called mancalas. Each player gets one.

One player picks up four stones from a pocket. Moving to the left, he drops one stone in each pocket. He drops the last stone in his mancala. The other player does the same. At the end, the mancala with the most stones wins!

People in China, North Korea, South Korea and Japan play Go. Two players sit around a square board. The board has **grid** lines. Each player has white or black stones. Stones are worth points.

The game starts with an empty board. Players take turns placing stones where lines cross. Players try to surround each other's stones. This is called **capturing**. Stones that haven't been captured give the player points. Captured stones take points away. The player with the most points wins.

People everywhere play games together. In many countries, they play tag. In Ghana, children play pilolo. People in Japan play Go. What games do you want to play?

MAP

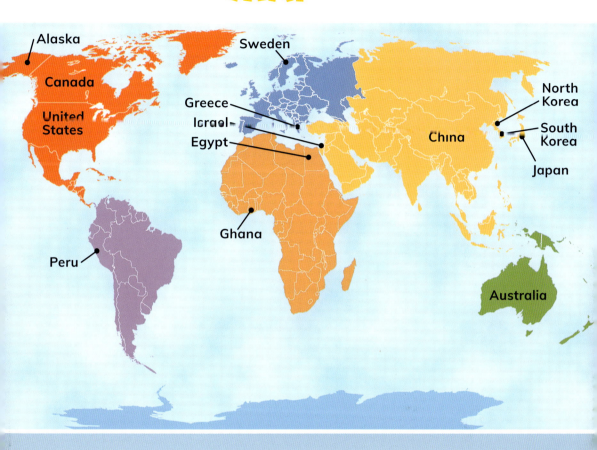

Around the world, people play different games. See which places were talked about in this book!

GLOSSARY

capture completely surround the other player's stone in the game of Go; captured stones take points away from the stone's original player

challenge test a person's skills

competition event where people try to win

divide separate into parts or groups

grid pattern of evenly spaced, or parallel, lines that cross

practise keep working to become better at a skill

stone wood-like covering around a seed found in the middle of some types of fruit

strategy plan for winning a game

FIND OUT MORE

BOOKS

Children Just Like Me: A New Celebration of Children Around the World, DK (DK Children, 2016)

Fascinating Role-Playing Games (Cool Competitions), Lori Jean Polydoros (Raintree, 2017)

Games Around the World (Engage Literacy), Kelly Gaffney (Raintree, 2020)

The History of Gaming (Video Game Revolution), Heather E. Schwartz (Raintree, 2020)

WEBSITES

www.bbc.co.uk/bitesize/collections/primary-games/1
Try these fun games!

www.dkfindout.com/uk/history/victorian-britain/childrens-games-and-toys
Find out about Victorian children's games and toys.

www.dkfindout.com/uk/sports
Learn more about different sports from around the world.

INDEX

agalmata 8
Alaska 22
Australia 12

board games 24, 26

Canada 22
capturing 26
catch the dragon's tail 6
China 6, 26
competitions 22

down down down 12–13

Egypt 24

families 4
friends 4, 16

Ghana 18, 28
Go 26, 28
go-go-im 11
go-gos 10, 11
Greece 8

hide-and-seek 16

Inuit 22
Israel 10

Japan 26, 28

mancala 24

North Korea 26

Peru 14
pilolo 18, 28

sapo 14
searching 16, 18
skills 4
South Korea 26
sport 20, 22
stick pull 22
strategies 24
Sweden 20

table tennis 20
tag 6, 8, 28
throwing 10, 11, 12, 14

United States 16